# shots

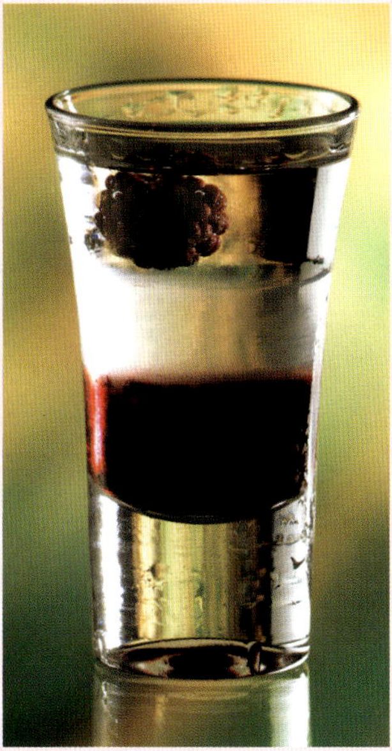

This is a Parragon book
First published in 2006

Parragon
Queen Street House
4 Queen Street
Bath BA1 1HE, UK



ISBN 1-40547-316-9



Printed in China

**WARNING**

Recipes using raw eggs are not suitable for children, the elderly, pregnant women, convalescents and anyone suffering from an illness. Please consume alcohol sensibly.

# contents

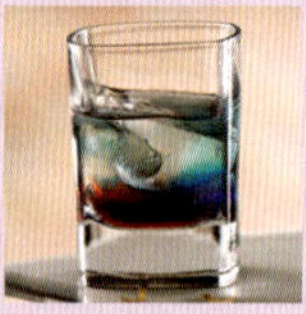

# firelighter

If you are really looking for a cocktail to give you a kick, this is it. The infamous absinthe is a seriously strong spirit and not to be treated lightly!

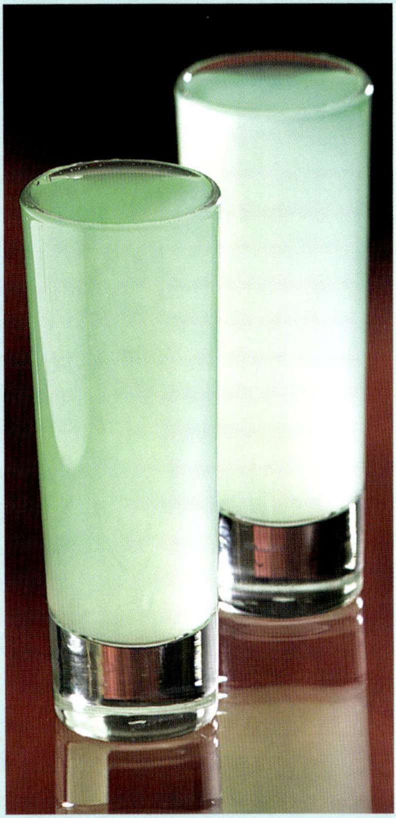

**SERVES 1**

1 measure absinthe, iced
1 measure lime juice cordial, iced

**1** Ice a shot glass.
**2** Shake the absinthe and lime over ice and, when well frosted, strain into the shot glass.

# tequila slammer

Slammers are also known as shooters. The idea is that you pour the ingredients directly into the glass, without stirring. Cover the glass with one hand to prevent spillage, slam it on to a table to mix and drink the cocktail down in one! Do ensure you use a strong glass!

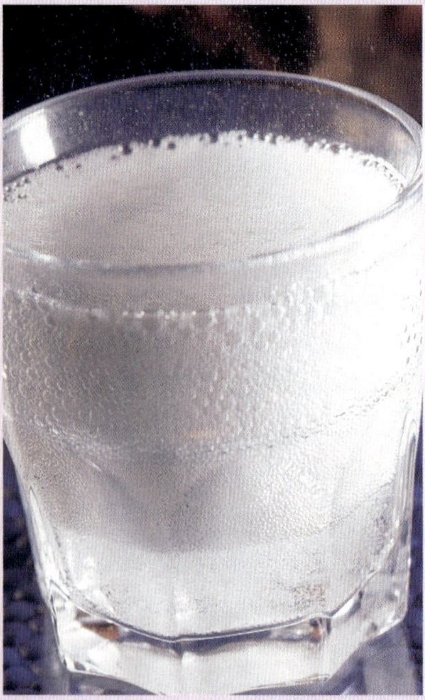

**SERVES 1**

1 measure white tequila, chilled
1 measure lemon juice
sparkling wine, chilled

**1** Put the tequila and lemon juice into a chilled glass.
**2** Top up with sparkling wine.
**3** Cover the glass with your hand and slam.

# angel's delight

This is a modern version of the classic pousse-café, an unmixed, mixed drink, in that the ingredients form separate layers in the glass – providing you have a steady hand – to create a rainbow effect. You can drink it as a slammer or sip it.

**SERVES 1**

- ½ measure chilled grenadine
- ½ measure chilled Triple Sec
- ½ measure chilled sloe gin
- ½ measure chilled single cream

**1** Pour the grenadine into a chilled shot glass, pousse-café glass or champagne flute, then, with a steady hand, pour in the Triple Sec to make a second layer.
**2** Add the sloe gin to make a third layer and, finally, add the cream to float on top.

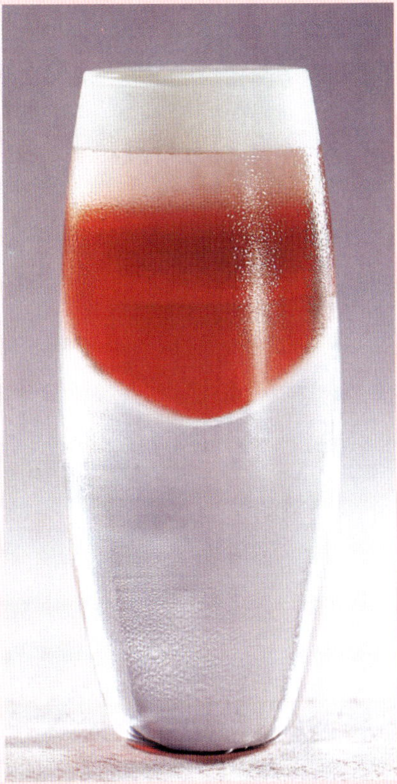

# russian double

Vodka and schnapps are both very strong drinks, so handle with care!

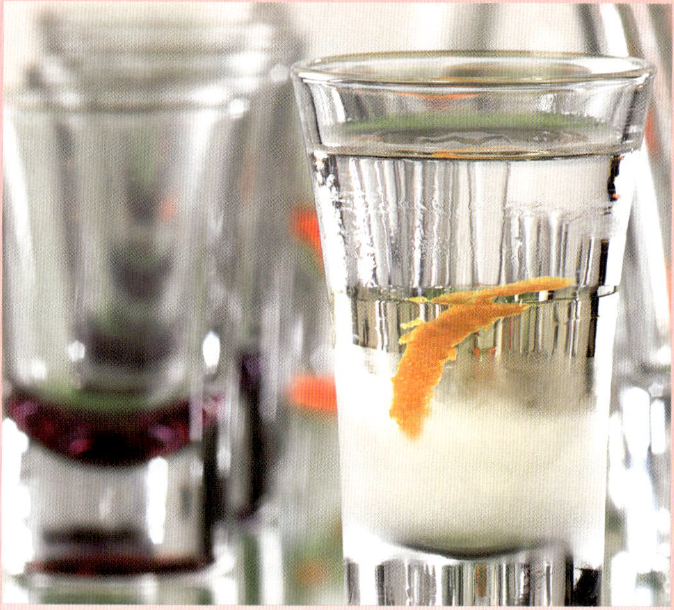

**SERVES 1**

1 measure vodka, iced
strips of lemon or orange peel
1 measure lemon vodka or schnapps, iced

**1** Layer the drinks carefully, putting a piece of peel in the first layer, in a chilled shot glass and drink immediately.

# aurora borealis

Like a pousse-café, this spectacular coloured drink should not be mixed or stirred. Leave it to swirl around the glass, creating a multi-hued effect and try to guess the various flavours.

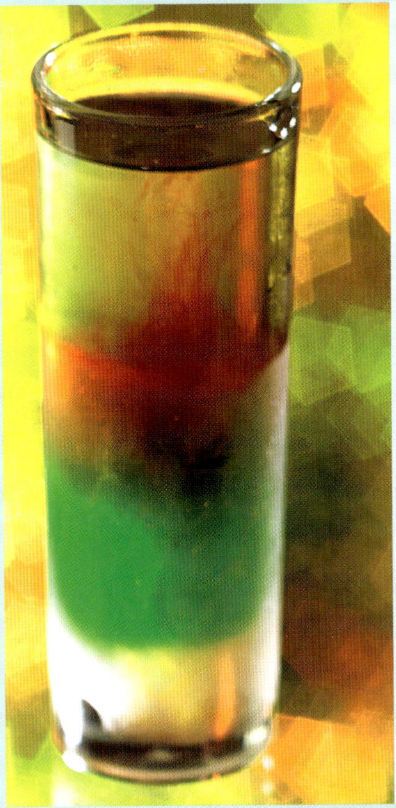

**SERVES 1**

1 measure iced grappa or vodka

1 measure iced green Chartreuse

½ measure iced orange Curaçao

few drops iced cassis

**1** Pour the grappa slowly round one side of a well-chilled shot glass.

**2** Gently pour the Chartreuse round the other side.

**3** Pour the Curaçao gently into the middle and add a few drops of cassis just before serving. Don't stir. Drink slowly!

# sputnik

If you are making several of these they can be prepared in advance ready with different coloured cherries on top in orbit.

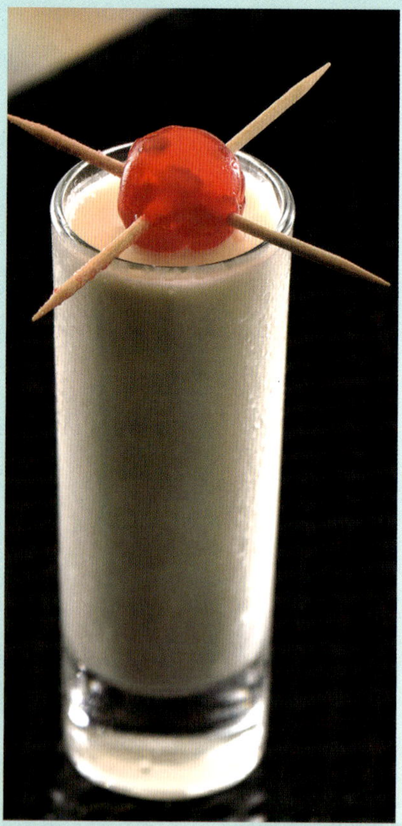

**SERVES 1**

1 measure vodka
1 measure cream
1 tsp maraschino
ice
maraschino cherry

**1** Shake all the ingredients well over ice and strain into a shot glass.
**2** Finish with a cherry supported on 2 or more diagonal cocktail sticks.

# perfect love

This is the literal translation for an unusual purple liqueur flavoured with rose petals, almonds and vanilla.

**SERVES 1**

1 measure vodka
½ measure Parfait Amour
½ measure maraschino
scoop crushed ice

**1** Shake all the ingredients together over ice until frosted.

**2** Strain into a chilled shot glass with more ice.

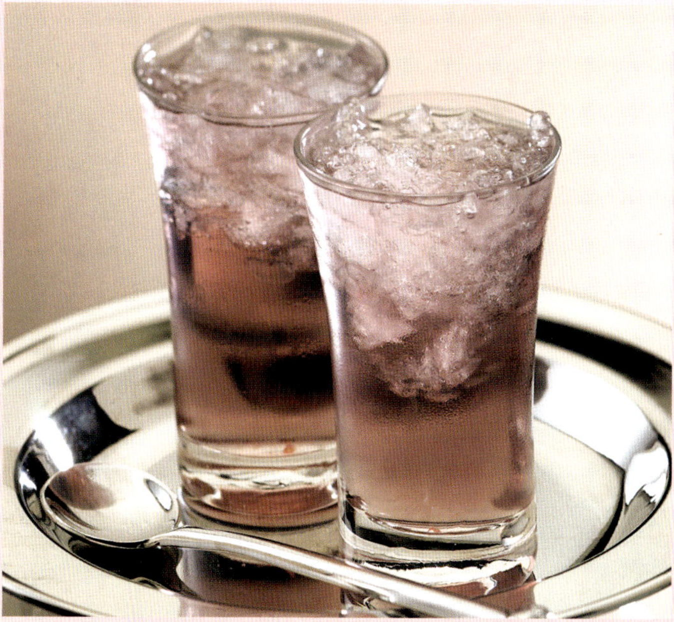

# anouchka

Sambuca is liquorice-flavoured and therefore not to everyone's taste. However, used here with a dash of blackberry liqueur and the iced vodka, it's a great combination.

**SERVES 1**

1 measure vodka, iced
dash black Sambuca
dash crème de mure
a few blackberries

**1** Pour the vodka into a chilled shot glass.
**2** Add a dash of the Sambuca and then a dash of the crème de mure.
**3** Dress with a few blackberries, fresh or frozen.

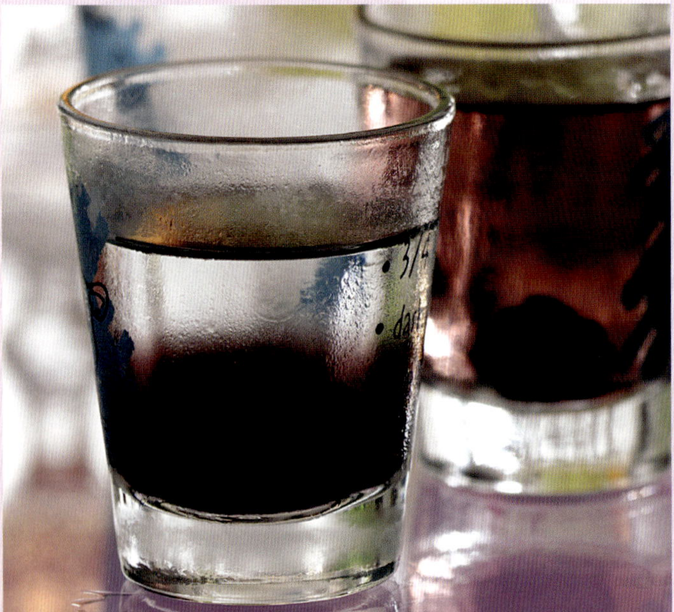

# silver berry

This drink is perfect for one of those very special occasions – except that you really can't drink very many!

**SERVES 1**

1 measure raspberry vodka, iced
1 measure crème de cassis, iced
1 measure Cointreau, iced
edible silver paper or a frozen berry

**1** Carefully and slowly layer the ingredients, in the order listed, in a well-iced shot glass.
**2** They must be well iced first and may need time to settle into their layers.
**3** Dress with the silver paper or a frozen berry.

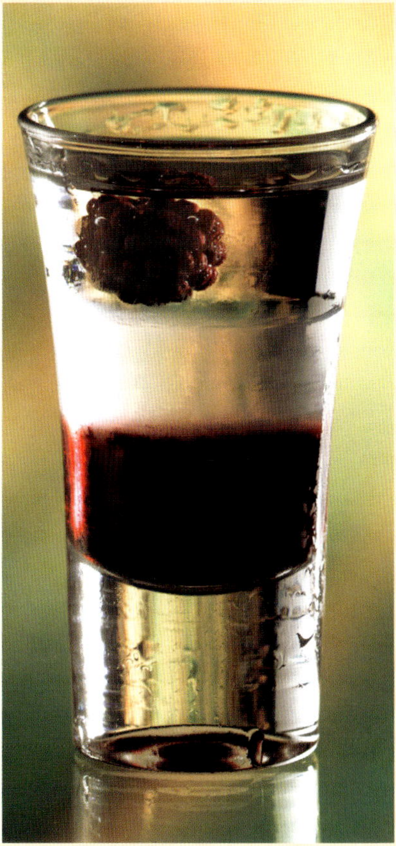

# depth charge

Anise is a particularly unusual drink in that it turns cloudy when mixed with water but not when mixed with other alcoholic drinks, until the ice starts melting. So drink it slowly, with care, and watch it change.

**SERVES 1**

1 measure gin
1 measure Lillet
2 dashes Pernod
ice

**1** Shake all the ingredients over ice until well frosted.
**2** Strain into a chilled shot glass.

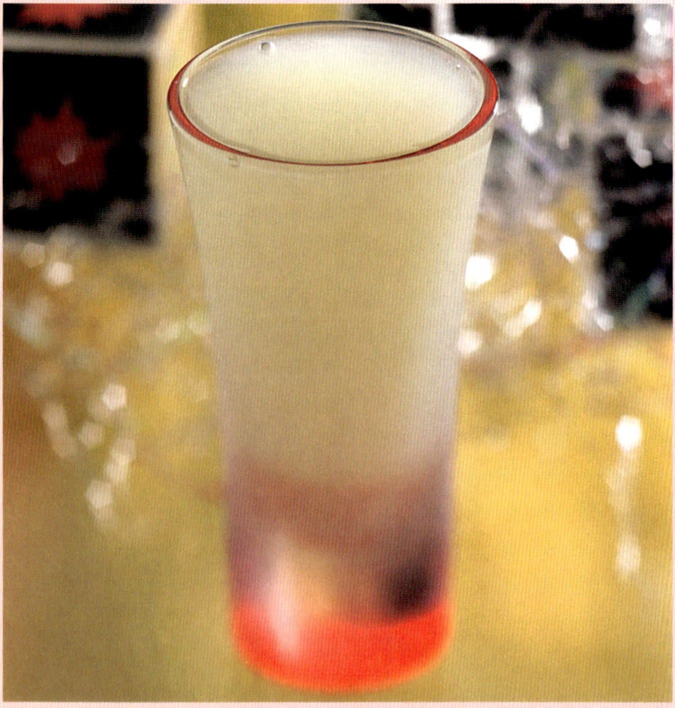

# peach floyd

Shots look stunning in the right type of glass, but as they are for drinking down in one, keep them small and have everything really well chilled.

**SERVES 1**

1 measure peach schnapps, chilled
1 measure vodka, chilled
1 measure white cranberry and peach juice, chilled
1 measure cranberry juice, chilled

**1** Stir all the ingredients together over ice and strain into an iced shot glass.

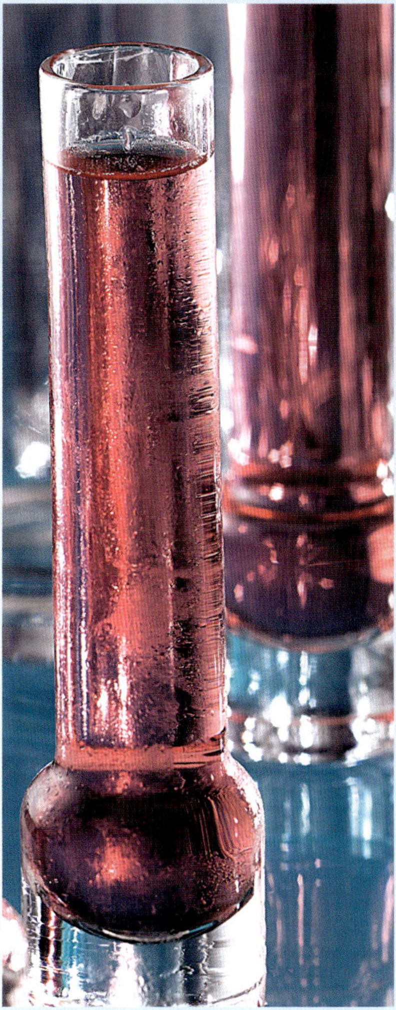

# high flyer

These two unusual liqueurs give a very aromatic and fruity cocktail.

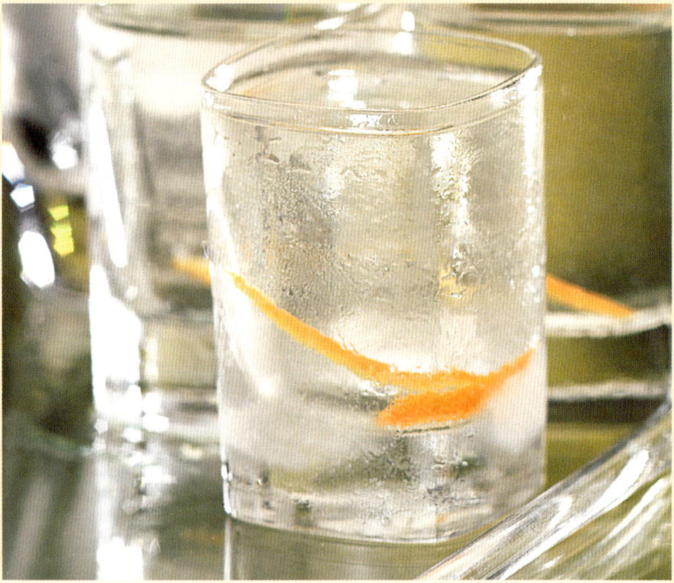

**SERVES 1**

⅔ measure gin
½ measure Strega
½ measure Van der Hum
or Triple Sec
ice
orange or lemon peel

**1** Stir the ingredients well over ice and strain into a shot glass.
**2** Finish with a twist of peel.

# nuclear fallout

This is similar to a pousse-café, where the liqueurs are layered, but, in this case, the heaviest liqueur is coldest and added last, to create the slow dropping effect!

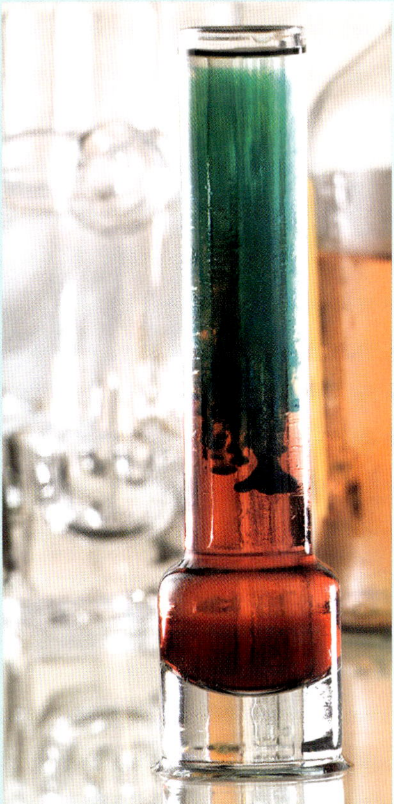

**SERVES 1**

1 tsp raspberry syrup
¼ measure of maraschino
¼ measure of yellow Chartreuse
¼ measure Cointreau
½ measure well-iced blue Curaçao

**1** Chill all the liqueurs but specifically putting the blue Curaçao in the coldest part of the freezer. Also chill a shot, pousse-café or elgin glass.
**2** Carefully pour the drinks, except the blue Curaçao, in layers over the back of a teaspoon.
**3** Finally, pour in the blue Curaçao and wait for the fallout!

# pousse-café 81

A pousse-café is a layered cocktail of many different coloured liqueurs. It is crucial to ice all the liqueurs first.

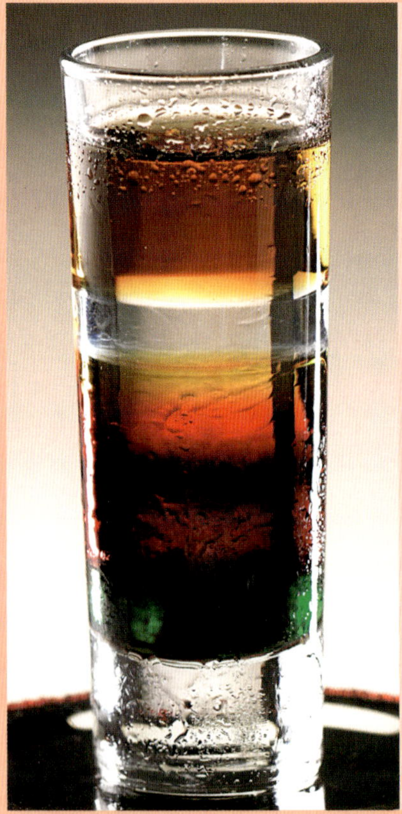

**SERVES 1**

- ¼ measure grenadine
- ¼ measure crème de menthe
- ¼ measure Galliano
- ¼ measure kümmel
- ¼ measure brandy

**1** Ice all the liqueurs and a tall shot, elgin or pousse-café glass.
**2** Carefully pour the liqueurs over a spoon evenly into the glass.
**3** Leave for a few minutes to settle.

# tornado

If the ingredients are really well iced, you will certainly create a tornado in your glass when you pour one into the other – just sit and watch them swirling for a moment!

**SERVES 1**

1 measure peach or other favourite schnapps, frozen
1 measure black Sambuca, frozen

**1** Pour the schnapps into an iced shot glass.
**2** Then gently pour on the Sambuca over the back of a spoon.
**3** Leave the shot for a few minutes to settle and separate before you down it.

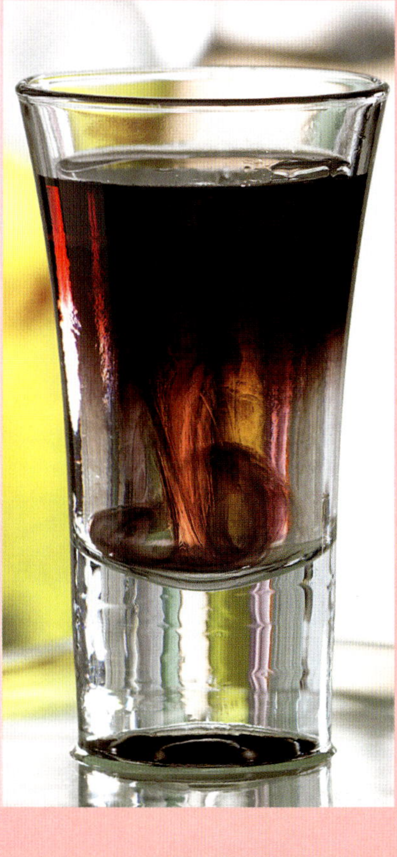

# stars and swirls

You will need a steady hand for this one – preferably two pairs of steady hands.

**SERVES 1**

1 measure Malibu
½ measure strawberry or raspberry liqueur
1 tsp blue Curaçao
ice

**1** Chill a small shot glass really well.
**2** Pour in the Malibu and add a large ice cube.
**3** Carefully pour in the other two liqueurs from opposite sides of the glass very slowly so they fall down the sides and swirl around.

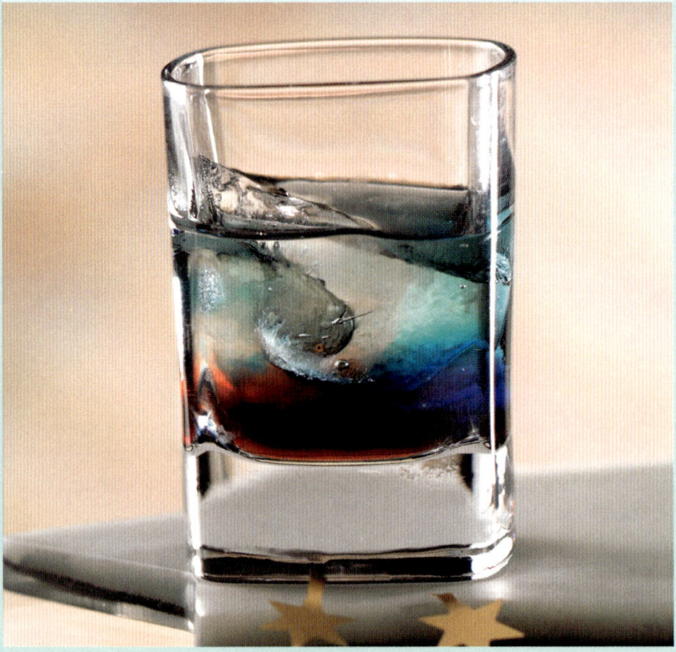

# toffee split

You should not need a dessert as well, but you could always pour it over some ice cream.

**SERVES 1**

1 measure toffee liqueur, iced
2 measures Drambuie
crushed ice

**1** Fill a small cocktail glass or shot glass with crushed ice.
**2** Pour on the Drambuie and pour in the toffee liqueur carefully from the side of the glass so it layers on top.
**3** Drink immediately.

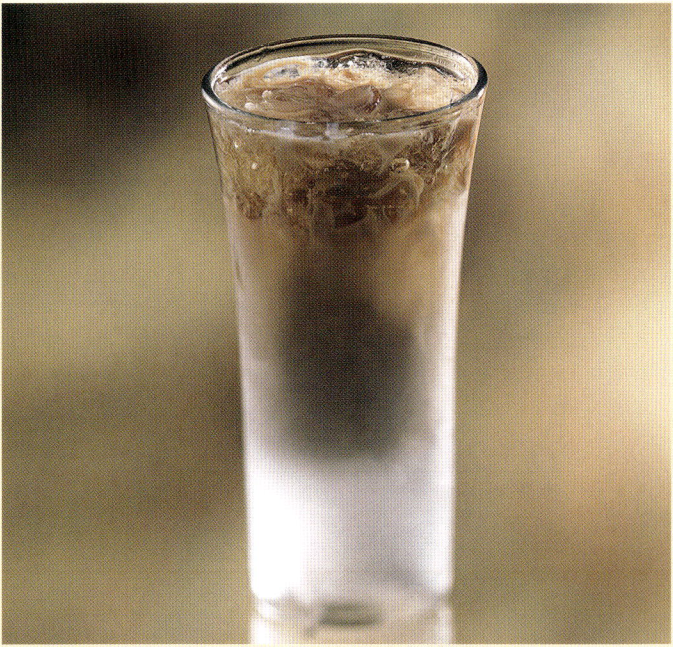

# white diamond frappé

This is a crazy combination of liqueurs, but it works well once you've added the lemon. Extra crushed ice at the last minute brings out all the separate flavours.

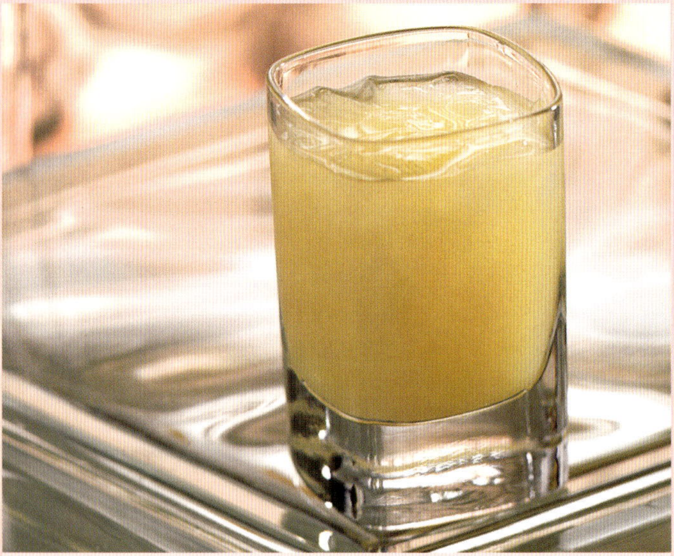

**SERVES 1**

¼ measure peppermint schnapps
¼ measure white crème de cacao
¼ measure anise liqueur
¼ measure lemon juice
ice

**1** Shake all the ingredients over ice until frosted.
**2** Strain into a chilled shot glass and add a small spoonful of crushed ice.

# banana bomber

This cocktail is as dazzling as it is delicious and gloriously addictive. Try it with white crème de cacao and a layer of cream too – equally irresistible!

**SERVES 1**

1 measure banana liqueur
1 measure brandy

**1** Pour the banana liqueur gently into a shot glass.
**2** Gently pour in the brandy over the back of a teaspoon, taking care not to let the layers mix.

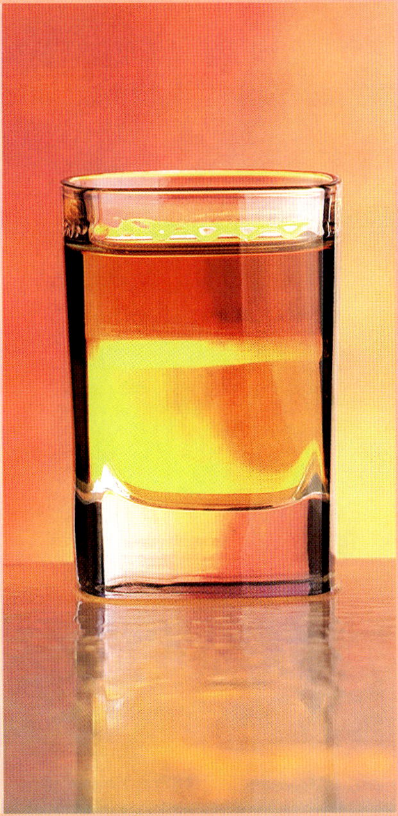

# loch lomond

Syrup de gomme was used long before we had mixers like ginger beer or tonic, so this may be where the idea stemmed from.

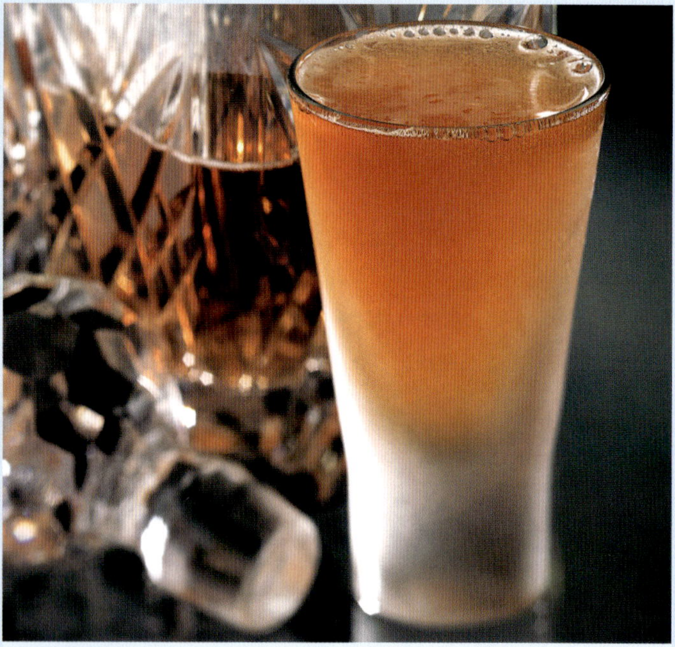

**SERVES 1**

1½ measures Scotch whisky
1 measure syrup de gomme
3 dashes Angostura bitters
ice

**1** Shake well over ice and strain into a shot glass.

# fancy free

The key to this layered drink is to ice the liqueur and ice the glass. If it does seem to mix on impact, give it a little time to settle and form its layers again.

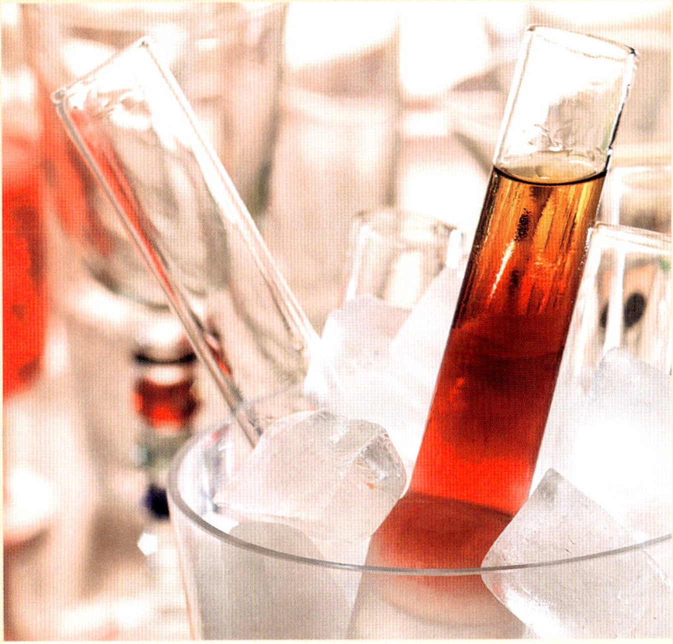

**SERVES 1**

⅓ measure cherry brandy, iced
⅓ measure Cointreau, iced
⅓ measure apricot liqueur, iced

**1** Pour the three liqueurs in order into an iced elgin, tall shot glass or liqueur glass. Pour them over the back of a spoon so they form coloured layers.

# jealousy

This really is an after-dinner cocktail and if you want a change, you could occasionally flavour the cream with a different liqueur.

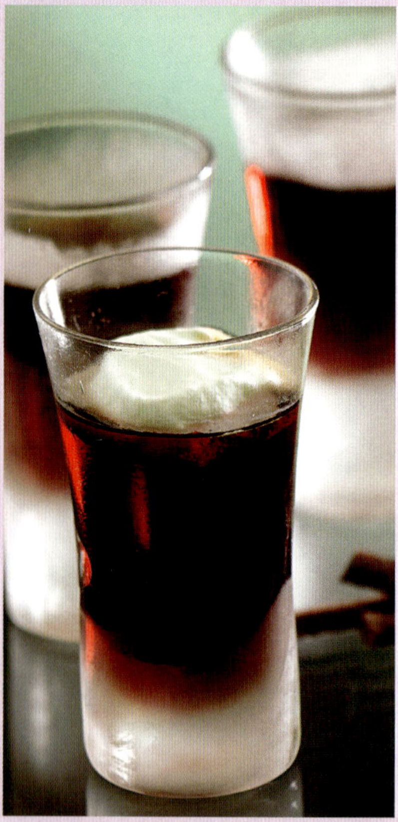

**SERVES 1**

1 tsp crème de menthe
1-2 tbsp double cream
2 measures coffee or chocolate liqueur
crushed ice
chocolate matchsticks

**1** Gently beat the mint liqueur into the cream until thick.
**2** Pour the coffee liqueur into an iced shot glass and carefully spoon on the flavoured whipped cream.
**3** Serve with chocolate matchsticks.

# katrina

You can use green mint liqueur if you prefer, but this one is prettier and tastes just as good.

**SERVES 1**

1 measure Galliano
½ measure white crème de menthe
½ measure brandy
ice

**1** Shake the first three ingredients well over ice.
**2** Strain into chilled shot glasses.

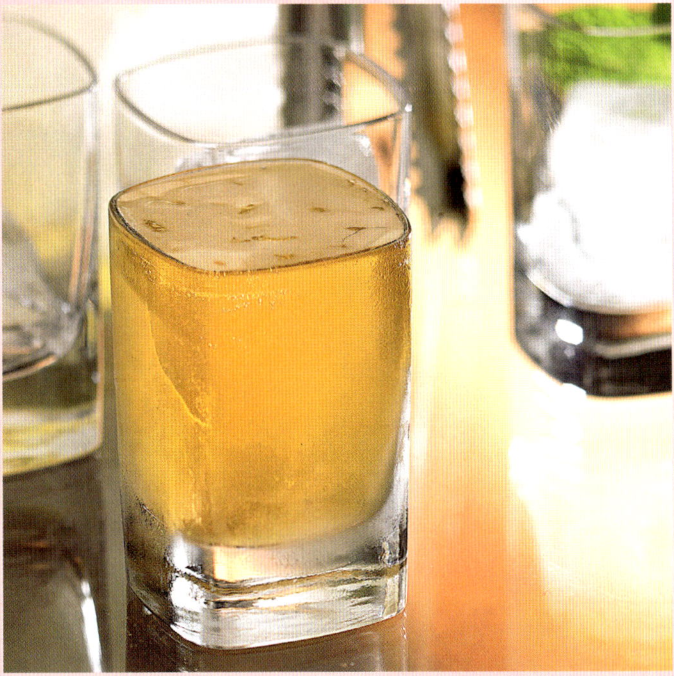

# fifth avenue

After-dinner cocktails often include cream and this one also has the delicate flavours of apricot and cocoa.

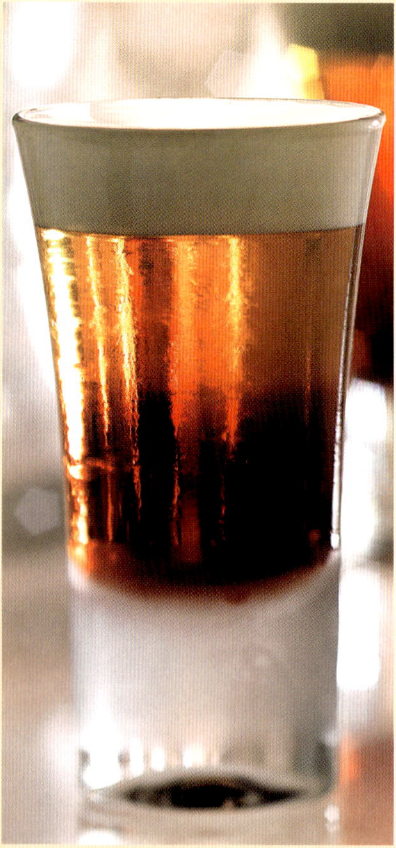

**SERVES 1**

1 measure dark crème de cacao, iced

1 measure apricot brandy, iced

1 measure cream

**1** Pour the ingredients, one at a time, into a chilled shot glass. Pour the layers slowly over the back of a spoon resting against the edge of the glass. Each layer should float on top of the previous one.

# african mint

Amarula is a very rich and exotic liqueur, which is best served and drunk really cold – but not on ice as that will dilute its real character.

**SERVES 1**

¾ measure crème de menthe, chilled
¾ measure Amarula, chilled

**1** Pour the crème de menthe into the base of a shot glass, saving a few drops.
**2** Pour the Amarula slowly over the back of a spoon to create a layer over the mint.
**3** Drizzle any remaining drops of mint over the creamy liqueur to finish.

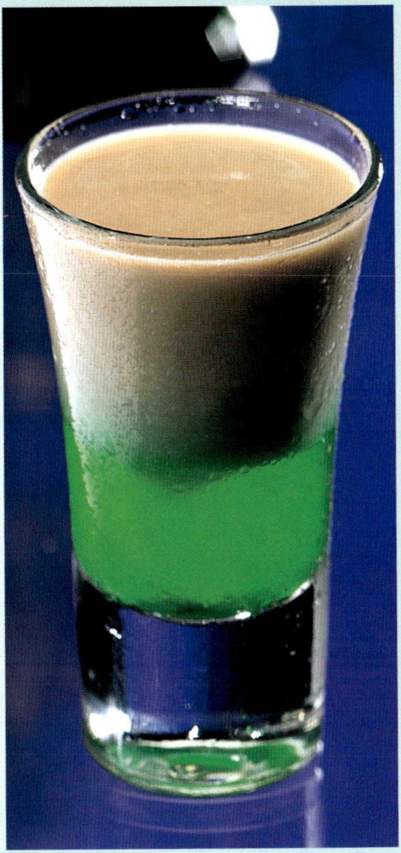

# napoleon's nightcap

Instead of hot chocolate, the French emperor Napoleon favoured a chocolate-laced brandy with a hint of banana and mint. Daring and extravagant!

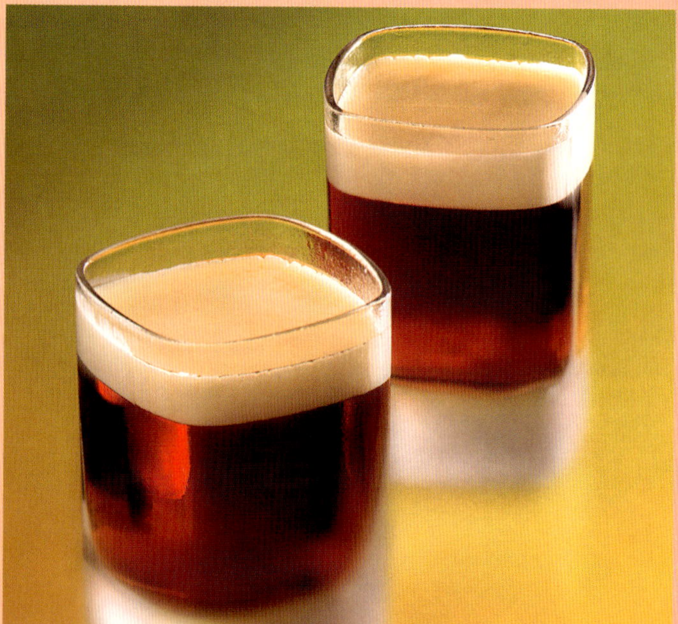

**SERVES 1**

1¼ measures cognac
1 measure dark crème de cacao
¼ measure crème de banane
1tbsp cream

**1** Stir the first three ingredients in a mixing glass with ice.
**2** Strain into a chilled shot glass and spoon on a layer of cream.

# alaska

Yellow Chartreuse is slightly sweeter than the green Chartreuse, so it does benefit from being really well chilled.

**SERVES 1**

½ measure gin
½ measure yellow Chartreuse
ice

**1** Shake the ingredients over ice until well frosted.
**2** Strain into a chilled shot glass.

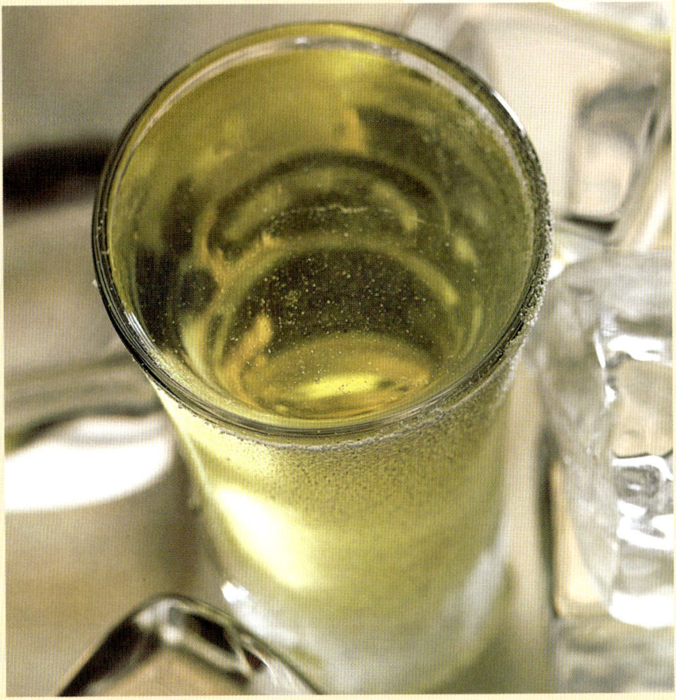

# prairie oyster

For times when you really can't lift your head off the pillow, it's the only thing to try.

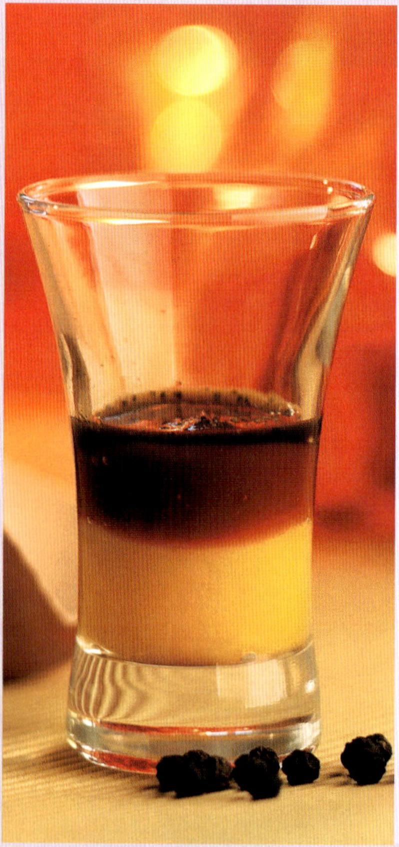

**SERVES 1**

Worcestershire sauce
vinegar
tomato ketchup
1 egg yolk
cayenne pepper

**1** Mix equal quantities of Worcestershire sauce, vinegar and ketchup and pour into a chilled glass.
**2** Add the yolk carefully without breaking.
**3** Do not stir, sprinkle with cayenne pepper and down it all in one!

# breakfast

It is difficult to believe that anyone would actually have the stomach to cope with drinking a shot first thing in the morning – but then, for those who party all night and sleep all day, cocktail time coincides with breakfast.

**SERVES 1**

2 measures gin
1 measure grenadine
cracked ice cubes
1 egg yolk

**1** Pour the gin and grenadine over ice in a shaker and add the egg yolk.
**2** Shake vigorously until frosted. Strain into a chilled shot glass.

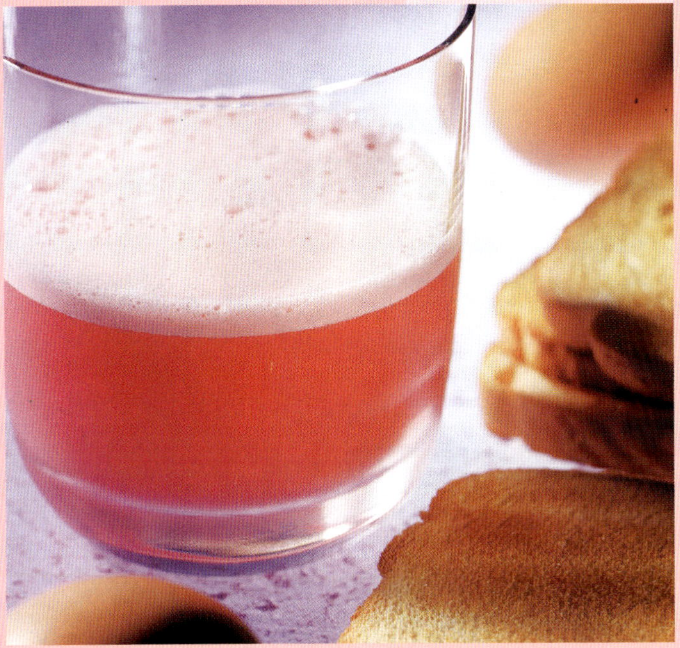

# hair of the dog

This well-known expression – a tot of whatever gave you the hangover – is in fact a popular Scottish 'morning after' tipple!

**SERVES 1**

1 measure Scotch whisky
1½ measures single cream
½ measure clear honey
ice

**1** Gently mix the whisky, cream and honey together.
**2** Pour into a shot glass over ice and serve with a straw.

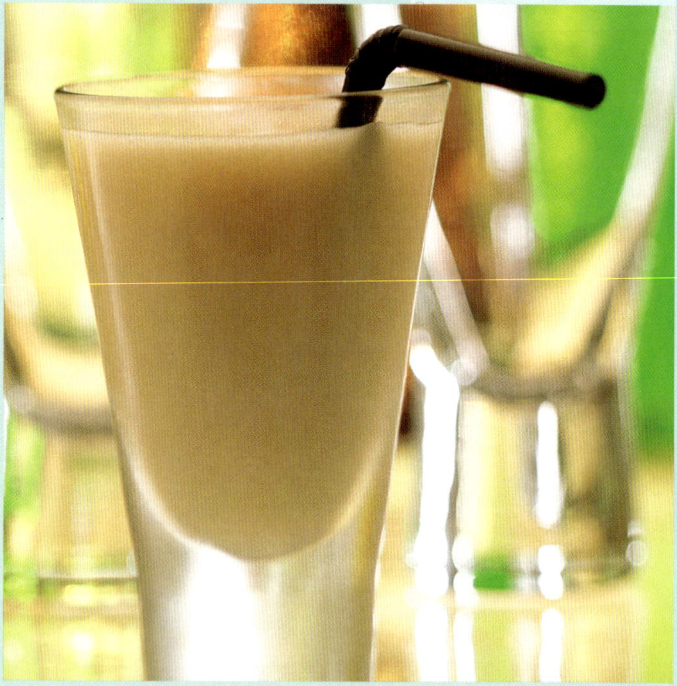